Ant's Diary

If found, please return this diary to:

NAME	Ant
ADDRESS	Under the paving slab by the pink flowers

Personal Details

SIZE	Smaller than this dot ●
OCCUPATION	Worker and Forager (food collector)
HOBBIES	Work
COLOURING	Almost Black, like all my friends
FAVOURITE FOOD	Honeydew and other sugary things
FAVOURITE WEATHER	Cool and damp

A Reader's Digest® Children's Book,
published 1999 by Reader's Digest Children's Publishing Ltd,
King's Court, Parsonage Lane, Bath BA1 1ER,
a subsidiary of The Reader's Digest Association, Inc.

Conceived, edited and designed by Tucker Slingsby Limited
Berkeley House, 73 Upper Richmond Road, London SW15 2SZ

ISBN 1-84088-097 X

Illustrations by Tim Hayward, Robin Carter and Adam Stower
Additional graphic manipulation by Adam Wilmott
Text by Steve Parker

Ant's Diary

with the help of

Steve Parker

••••••••

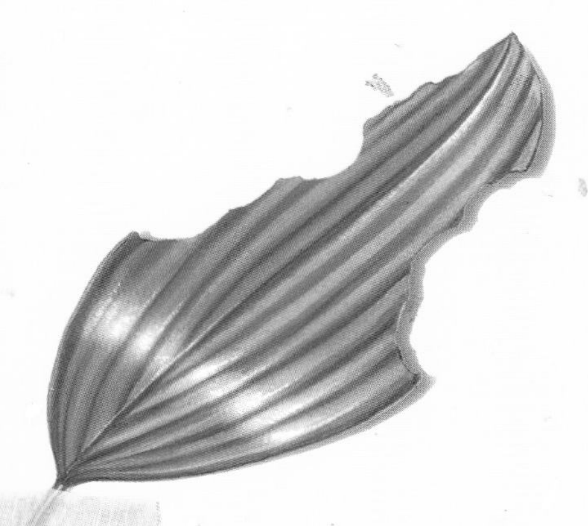

Reader's Digest
Children's Books

MEET ME

I've got a few minutes to spare, so I can begin my diary at last. Some of us have been given a short rest from work but, like all ants, I like to be busy, busy, busy, so here are a few facts about me and my friends.

All ants work very hard. We love it. Work is all we do and all we want to do. There's no time for playing. By the time I've worked, eaten and rested — it's time to work again. YIPPEE!

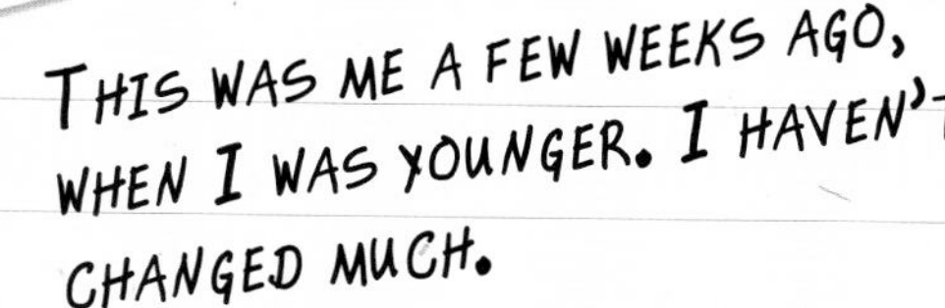

THIS WAS ME A FEW WEEKS AGO, WHEN I WAS YOUNGER. I HAVEN'T CHANGED MUCH.

ME AND MY NEST-MATES. WE ALL HAVE DIFFERENT JOBS TO DO. SOLDIERS GUARD OUR NEST, WORKERS KEEP THINGS NEAT AND TIDY AND FORAGERS LOOK FOR FOOD. WHEN I'M A BIT OLDER I'M GOING TO BE A FORAGER!

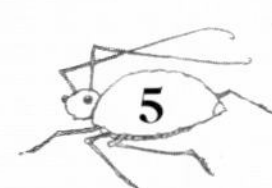

LIST OF THINGS I KNOW

- Ants are tiny.
- Ants' brains are even tinier. We don't have much room for learning but we are born knowing all we need to know – how to work.
- Ants are ~~inseets~~ ~~insetes~~ ~~isneets~~ INSECTS.

I found all this out from 'Old Ant', our oldest and wisest sister, who knows EVERYTHING! Old Ant let me nibble some pages out of a book she found, which explains it all. I've stuck some of the pages in my diary.

Rest period over – I'm on duty again. HOORAY – back to work!

Insects of the world:

- There are more kinds of insects than all other animals added together – over one million.
- The biggest insects are moths and butterflies with wings 25 centimetres across, stick insects 30 centimetres long, and goliath beetles weighing 100 grams.
- Other kinds of insects are ants, ← ME! bees, wasps, flies, grasshoppers and crickets, dragonflies, cockroaches, earwigs, lacewings, bugs and fleas.

A Grasshopper

A Moth

- A typical insect has six legs and three body parts – a head, a thorax and an abdomen.

ME – BY ME

MY ANTENNAE (FEELERS) – FOR FEELING, SMELLING, TASTING AND TAPPING

MY EYES – FOR SEEING

MY JAWS – FOR CUTTING UP FOOD AND HOLDING ONTO THINGS

MY ABDOMEN – MY FOOD GOES IN HERE AFTER I'VE EATEN IT

MY LEGS – FOR WALKING

THERE ARE MILLIONS AND MILLIONS OF ANTS IN THE WORLD - MORE ANTS THAN PEOPLE. SO ALTHOUGH WE'RE TINY - I THINK WE'RE VERY IMPORTANT!

FRIENDS ON THE INTERNEST

All my nest-mates look quite, in fact very, like me. But I've got other ant friends too. Here are some pictures they've sent me by post and on the Internest. They live in nests far away from my paving slab, and their lives sound very exciting! Like me, they are all busy, busy, busy.

BITER

Look at those jaws! Biter's a Bulldog Ant — she lives in Australia. When her nest is attacked, Biter uses those huge, strong jaws to bite her enemies. They sound pretty useful to me!

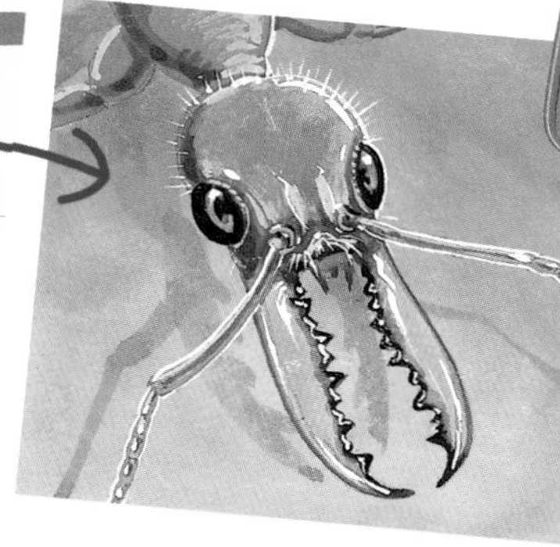

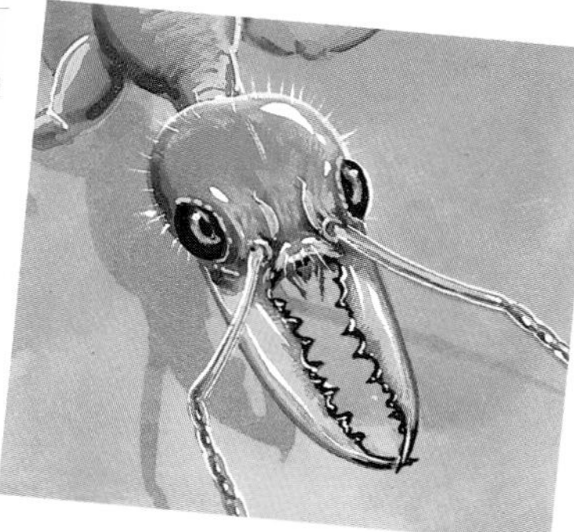

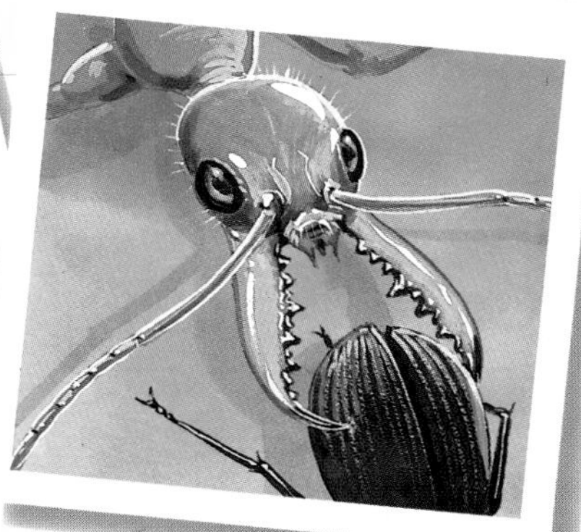

SWEETS

My favourite penpal! She's a Honeypot Ant from North America. She's sweet, gooey and fat. Her abdomen is full of a sticky, sugary liquid. When her sisters stroke her, she oozes a bit of the liquid for them to drink. I bet it tastes nice!

Termite mounds on the African Savanna

BLANCO

This postcard is from my friend Blanco who's not really an ant at all — she's a Termite. You can see her nest on the left. It's really tall — much bigger than my Nest. She lives there with millions of her sisters. The nest is in Africa, which is very hot and dry, and Blanco is very soft and white (not hard and black like me). But she's a sensible termite and spends most of her time in the dark, damp nest, away from the baking hot sun.

JAWS

Jaws is a full-time Soldier Ant. She and her friends defend their nest from enemies who want to eat their eggs and grubs. Soldier Ants have much bigger heads and jaws than me. THEY'RE FIERCE!

UCY

ucy is called a Leaf-cutter Ant ecause she cuts off pieces of eaf with her jaws and carries hem like a sunshade — so do all er friends! I must look in Old Ant's book to see if I can find ut why.

THAT'S LUCY

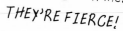

Where I Live

Another break, and a chance to write about our Nest. It's big with lots of tunnels and loads of chambers. The roof is huge and hard and flat. Inside, it's LOVELY — dark, cool and damp! And it's very busy, with lots and lots of nest-mates scurrying everywhere. Each of us has learnt our way about from a map we're given when we become adults.

I've never been Outside. But I'm on the list to be a Forager so I should go out soon — EXCITING! Outside is where food comes from. Old Ant says it's even bigger than our Nest. Some nest-mates say Outside is dark, like the Nest, but others say it's light and sunny. I can't wait to find out!

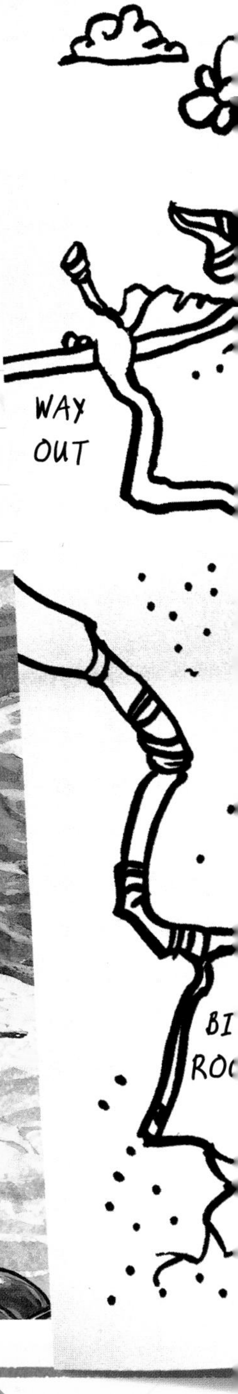

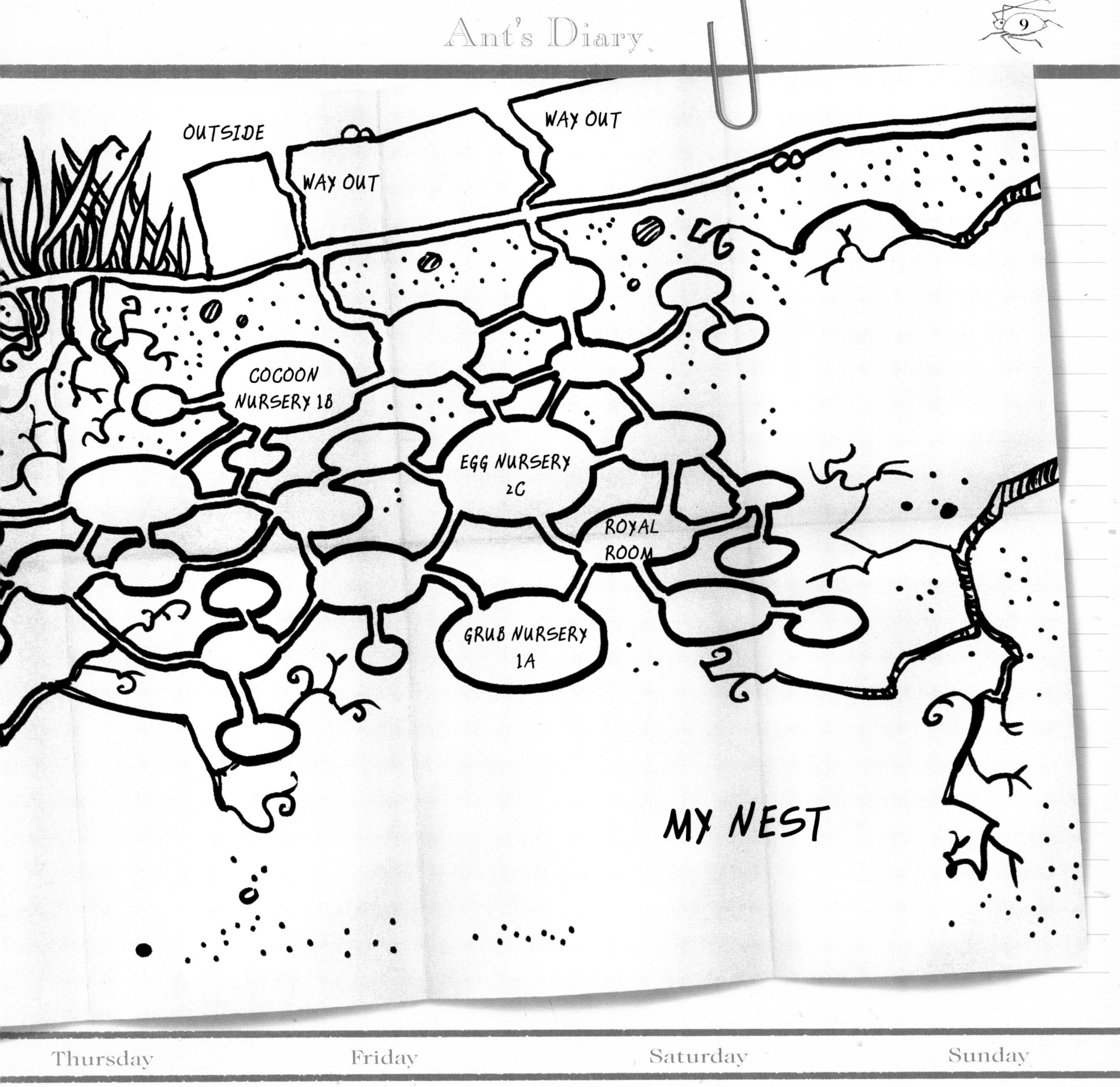

Thursday Friday Saturday Sunday

VISIT TO THE NURSERY

I've just seen the Queen! She's my Mum. She's also Mum to almost all of my nest-mates. Our Dad died ages ago, even before Old Ant hatched, and she must be the oldest ant in the nest (apart from the Queen, of course!).

The Queen is ENORMOUS! She only has one job — laying eggs — and she's very busy. She lies in her Royal Room and lays dozens of eggs an hour. My job today was taking the eggs to the Nursery.

Last time, I was allowed to feed the Queen. Next time I hope to be allowed to clean away her droppings. What an honour!

WORK TO BE DONE BEFORE FIRST REST BREAK

Check eggs in Egg Nursery 2C.
Count grubs in Grub Nursery 1A.
See if cocoons in Cocoon Nursery 1B have changed into grown-ups.

MY MUM, THE QUEEN (SHE'S IN THE MIDDLE)

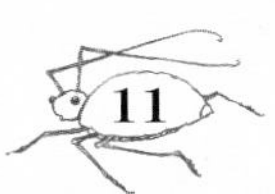

Thursday Friday Saturday Sunday

GROWING UP

There are always babies in the Nest. First they turn into grubs, then cocoons and finally into ants, just like me. Old Ant says this is called metamorphosis. All my nest-mates are female. Male ants appear later, at breeding time. The Queen is our Mum — so we're all sisters.

EGG FIRST!

Today I was busy checking the nurseries - it reminded me of when I was a grub. I started off life as an egg in Egg Nursery 1A. I was small, round and creamy white. Being an egg is a bit boring — you don't do anything!

GREEDY GRUBS

Next I hatched into a grub and I was always hungry! Once the eggs in my group had all hatched, they renamed our room Grub Nursery 1A. We all wriggled, grew lots bigger, shed our skins and ate all the time. The adult ants on nursery duty were always rushed off their feet. They called us larvae!

Food for the Fish

Give the fish in your pond a treat; feed them ants' eggs. They are nutritious and can be dug up in your garden.

Stupid, STUPID! They're COCOONS NOT EGGS!

TERRIBLE NEWS! SO MANY COCOONS BEING EATEN!

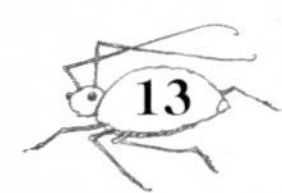

COSY, LAZY COCOONS

I can remember feeling quite exhausted after all that eating. All of us grubs then turned into cocoons. I can't remember much about this stage. I think I just rested — without eating any more food. Old Ant says that cocoons are really called ~~pupea~~ pupae.

THE BIG DAY

This picture shows me just minutes after breaking out of my cocoon! At last I was a grown-up ant. I was handed a map of the Nest and a list of jobs and duties. I felt VERY important.

DRAWINGS - BY ME

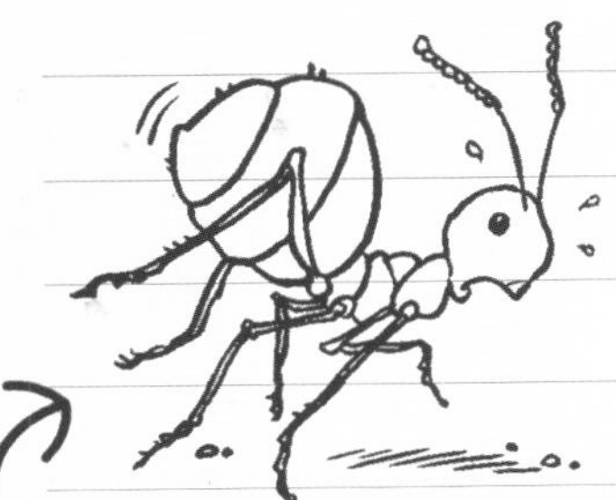

NEW ANT - JUST LIKE ME BUT SMALLER (A BIT CONFUSED BY ALL THE NEW JOBS AND DUTIES TO DO)

BUSY NURSERY ANT TURNING GRUB OVER.

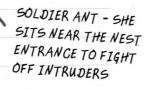

SOLDIER ANT - SHE SITS NEAR THE NEST ENTRANCE TO FIGHT OFF INTRUDERS

ANOTHER BUSY, BUSY DAY

Today, I've been working in the nursery. I've had so many jobs! Here's what I did . . .

I fanned some eggs by waving my antennae and legs, to keep them cool. The Nest is very warm now. It seems to get warm, then cool, then warm again, and so on. Old Ant says it's called 'day' and 'night'.

I cleaned, rolled and turned some eggs to make sure they won't go mouldy and die.

I moved some eggs from one chamber to another. A group of Workers is going to make the old chamber bigger because our Nest is getting too crowded.

I cleared away moulted skins. Grubs shed their skins a lot, especially when they turn into cocoons.

I cleaned up some grubby grubs and carried away their droppings.

I fed some grubs. They eat a sticky soup made from all kinds of things. We mix together leaf sap, the nectar from flowers, seeds and chewed-up worms. They grow very quickly on this tasty diet. YUM, YUM!

WHAT I'VE DONE

- Fanned eggs
- Cleaned and turned eg
- Moved eggs
- Tidied up moulted skin
- Mixed food
- Fed grubs
- Scrubbed grubs
- Cleaned droppings

EGG FANNING

TURNING EGGS

EGG MOVING

ME AND MY FELLOW WORKERS ON NURSERY DUTY. LOOK HOW BUSY, BUSY WE ARE! I THINK WE KEEP THE CLEANEST, TIDIEST NURSERY IN THE **WHOLE** WORLD!

TIDYING UP GRUB'S LAST MOULTED SKINS

IXING FOOD

GRUB-SCRUBBING

Thursday Friday Saturday Sunday

OUTSIDE AT LAST!

Wow! Today I followed a Forager and we went Outside! First, she tapped the ground with her antennae to pick up the Trail. This is a scent trail which the First Foragers put down as they go along. Old Ant calls the scent ~~feronone~~ pheromone. If we follow the scent trail, it leads us straight to the food, without getting lost.

First Foragers must be very BRAVE to go out and look for food. It's a jungle out there! The green strips, called grass, are so tall, I can't see their tops. There are great green slabs too, which take ages to walk across. They're called leaves. Outside was light and bright. Apparently, it'll get dark later on — weird! Old Ant says that's what day and night look like.

Thursday Friday Saturday Sunday

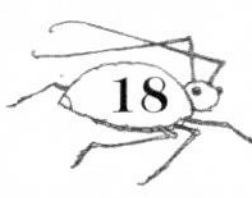

Giant Anteater

This long-nosed, long-tailed, long-haired mammal has a body one metre long. It lives in Central and South America. The Giant Anteater can rip open even the thickest ant-nest walls with its huge front claws. It eats about 10,000 ants each day, licking them up with its long, sticky tongue. But it only takes a few hundred ants from each nest, then moves to another. In this way the nests can be repaired and ready to yield more food a week or two later.

IT'S ENORMOUS!

ENEMY ATTACK!

Today was SO SCARY, I can hardly write! Ladybird came too near our Nest. She wanted to eat us, or carry away our grubs and cocoons. So, hundreds of my sisters and I all tapped our antennae and gave off our Alarm Scent. ATTACK THE ENEMY!

One group of Soldiers stood right in front of Ladybird. They tried to bite her. But she was biting back too. SHE CHOPPED ONE ANT IN HALF! Soldiers squirted something nasty called acid at Ladybird. They aimed their rear ends at her and fired the acid where it hurts — at Ladybird's eyes and antennae. It seemed to really sting her.

Still Ladybird didn't go! So more Soldiers ran round the back of her. They bit her legs and rear end, and squirted more acid. Ladybird soon realised our Nest was too big. There were too many of us. She gave up and crawled away. But I expect she'll be back.

After the battle, we were exhausted. Some of the older Soldiers explained about other enemies, and I drew pictures of them. I also found a picture of a terrifying, enormous ant-killer in Old Ant's book!

Thursday Friday Saturday Sunday

SPILLS AND THRILLS

Another exciting day! I went Outside again because the First Foragers had found a new source of food. Old Ant says it's called a picnic. On the grass, there were all kinds of yummy things. I'd never seen or tasted most of them before.

We sent signals back to the Nest — 'We need more Foragers!' Soon there were lots of us, scuttling around and snipping off bits of food to carry back to the Nest.

Some of the foods were horrible. The giant white sheet was dry, crunchy and tasteless. The shiny silver things were too hard to bite and almost too slippery to walk across. But other foods were lovely, especially the hard white sugar lumps. They taste a bit like the nectar we get from flowers.

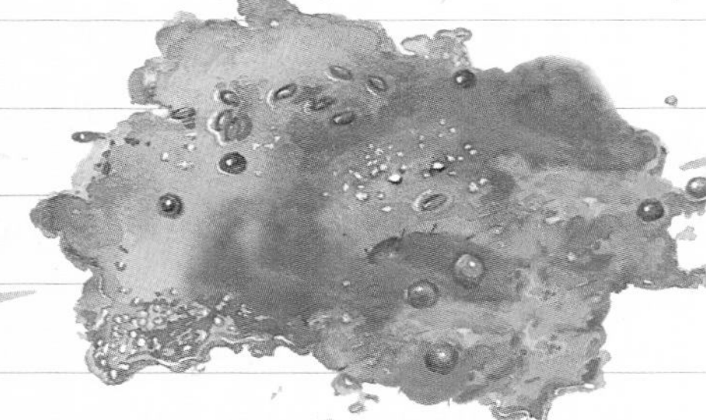

NEW FOODS I TRIED TODAY

I described the food to Old Ant, so I can now write down what I have eaten:

- Huge red balls with pale spots on them. Taste sweet and juicy. These are called strawberries.
- Bread — a giant white slab with small, spongy holes through it. It tastes slightly sweet, a bit like grass seeds.
- Pink flaky stuff on the bread. Tastes salty. Old Ant thinks it's tuna - a big fish, whatever that is!
- Jam sponge cake — DELICIOUS! Sweet, gooey stuff inside two crumbly layers.
- Great brownish ball, hard and slippery. Tastes sour, almost like the acid we squirt. It's called a pickled onion — UGGHHHH!

I BROUGHT THIS BLOB OF FRUITY JAM BACK BUT IT STUCK TO THE PAGE. WHEN NO-ONE'S LOOKING I CAN NIBBLE IT UP!

GUESTS IN THE NEST

I have been very busy today — taking a survey of the Nest. The Queen asked me to list all the Not-ants living with us at the moment. There are always lodgers and visitors down here. They like the dark and cool, too.

It's a good thing that I've got great antennae to help me feel my way around. Otherwise, in the dark, I couldn't find the Not-ants, or tap my nest-mates to talk to them.

Some Not-ants are stacks of trouble! One of the worst is Spider — she's big but hard to find. She moves in a sneaky, silent way and knows the nest backwards, inside-out and upside-down. She's even older than Old Ant!

WARNING

If you see these Not-ants, report to a Soldier at once. Do not approach — they could be dangerous.

SPIDER 
Very big and strong.
Eight legs, hairy body.
Poisonous bite.
Can trap you in sticky threads.
May carry off eggs, grubs or cocoons.

ROVE BEETLE 
Fairly big and strong.
Brown head, hairy yellow body.
Six legs, powerful jaws.
May carry off eggs, grubs or cocoons.

Some Not-ants, like Woodlouse, are no trouble. She eats old, empty cocoons, moulted skins from our grubs, empty ants' egg shells and even grub droppings. We have to pick up droppings when we're cleaning but we'd never eat them. Yuk! Still, in general, she helps to keep the Nest clean and tidy. I sometimes tap her with my antennae to say 'thank you'.

Our most favourite Not-ants are Aphids. But they live Outside on a Farm. I hope to visit them tomorrow.

HONEYDEW - YUM?! YUM!
(It's not very easy to draw)

MY FAVOURITE APHID

ON THE FARM

Today we went Outside with the Farmer Ants. We marched to a big plant covered with curious creatures called aphids. They have six legs like me but they're smaller, hairier and some are BRIGHT GREEN!

When you stroke an aphid, it oozes a sweet, sticky juice from its rear end! We call it HONEYDEW. It tastes delicious!

We get on well with aphids. They eat plants and make honeydew. We eat their honeydew and in return protect them from fierce aphid-eaters, like Ladybird. Sometimes ants get killed in the battles.

Later when we were full up, we went back to the Nest, sicked up some honeydew and shared it with the others. WHAT A PARTY!

Looking after aphids is hard work. Sometimes Farmer Ants have to move them to a safer place under a big leaf. But it takes AGES! Aphids are so slow and stupid. Not like us — we are quick, clever AND do what we're told!

Being a Farmer Ant is the most DANGEROUS job in the whole Nest. Luckily I only had to do the job for one day, and here I am, back safe and sound.

ANTS EAT MOULDY LEAVES!

Fungus, or Leaf-cutter, ants in North America live in gigantic nests in vast underground caves. The ants cut up leaves and bring them back to the nest. There they chew them and dampen them with spit and droppings. The leaf bits go mouldy and these odd ants eat the mould, called fungus.

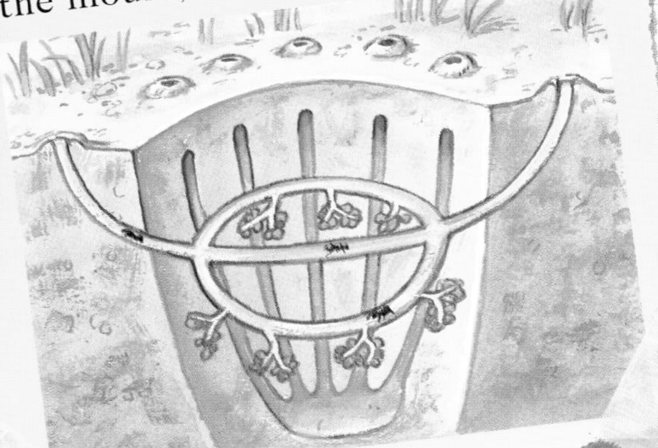

SO THAT'S WHAT LUCY DOES WITH THOSE LEAVES!

Thursday

Friday

Saturday

Sunday

SWARM IN THE WARM

Today was STRANGE! The Nest has been getting very crowded and then suddenly, lots of my nest-mates just left home.

I watched the last batch of grown-ups come out of their cocoons; there were sisters — and to my amazement, BROTHERS, TOO! The first male ants I've ever seen! Each new ant had four thin and flappy body parts. Old Ant called these things 'wings'.

The weather today has been hot and sticky. The Strange Winged Ants seemed to like it. First they stood at the nest entrances, then they flapped their wings and suddenly rose into the air. F-ANT-ASTIC! Old Ant says they will fly until they meet Winged Ants from other Nests. Then they will mate and breed. The male ants will die but the females, my sisters, will become Queen Ants and set up new Nests far away.

THESE THUNDERFLIES WERE EVERYWHERE TODAY. THEY'RE EVEN SMALLER THAN ME! THEY SEEM TO BRING THE THUNDER.

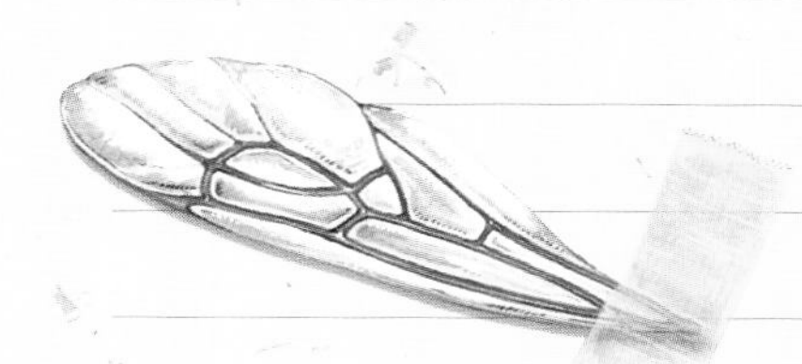

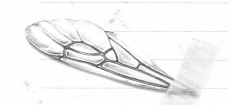

THIS WING FELL OFF ONE OF MY NEST-MATES. HE DIDN'T FLY FAR!

Thursday | Friday | Saturday | Sunday

THE GREAT DISASTER!

This is the first rest break I've had today. A great disaster has struck the Nest and I've had to work hard without stopping.

Just after the Strange Winged Ants went, there was a great storm. Usually, when it rains, a bit of water trickles into our Nest. Sister nest-workers soon mend any damage. But this time, the water POURED in. Water GUSHED through the tunnels and FLOODED the chambers. It was terrible — eggs, grubs and cocoons were SWEPT away. The nursery walls turned to mud and the ceilings fell in. Lots of Foragers and Nursery Workers were trapped and couldn't get out. The Nest was an awful mess!

But ants won't be beaten. We worked hard, rescued the eggs and grubs and cocoons, and started to repair the damaged walls. By tomorrow, the Nest will be back to normal.

EMERGENCY

Volunteers needed in all areas.
We must all work harder than ever to make the Nest fit for our Queen again.

YOUR NEST NEEDS YOU!

DAMAGE REPORT

Entrances	3-9 blocked.
Tunnels	6 and 20-39 collapsed.
Tunnels	14-15 filled with soil.
Tunnels	16 filled with stones.
Chambers	7-19 caved in.

BRAVERY AWARDS

To be awarded to 9 Nursery Workers for helping the Queen along the Escape Tunnel and saving her life.

SUN AGAIN

Yesterday was a difficult day. But now the sun's come out again and all the survivors are back doing their old jobs.

Old Ant slipped in a wet tunnel yesterday and hurt her leg. Well, she is very old and doesn't move as nippily as she used to. It happens to the best of us ants. We start walking instead of running everywhere. Then we need more and more rest breaks and start making mistakes. I think that soon Old Ant will rest forever.

When it happens, some of the others will look after her. Like all ants, she's always been very BUSY, BUSY so a long, long rest probably sounds wonderful to her. Me, I still have lots of work to do before my big rest — collecting nectar from the flowers is today's job.

The days are getting shorter and I think the dark, cold time that Old Ant warned us about will soon be here. She called it Winter. It's time to wrap up this diary carefully. Perhaps next year another ant will continue the story of our Nest. I've written about the Ladybird attack, the Strange Winged Ants leaving home, and the Great Flood. I wonder if the Nest will be as interesting next year.

MY FAVOURITE FLOWERS CAREFULLY PRESSED BY ANT

Geranium petal

Rose petal

Viola

Honeysuckle

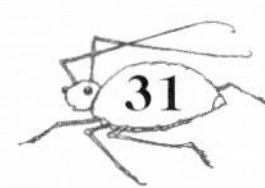

Thursday Friday Saturday Sunday

OLD ANT'S WISE WORDS

Old Ant has a huge memory. She knows at least 14 things! I wrote them down so that we'll know them too, even after she's gone off for her last rest.

ABDOMEN
The rear part of an ant's body, behind the bit with the legs. An ant's body is divided into three parts — the head, the thorax and the abdomen.

ADULT
The last and busy stage of an ant's life. A grown-up, with six legs — not an egg, grub or cocoon.

ANTENNAE
Feelers, two long thin parts on the head which we use for touching, smelling, tasting, tapping and talking.

COCOON
The third stage of an ant's life, after the grub, but before the adult. Also called the pupa (plural pupae).

EGG
The first stage of an ant's life. Eggs are laid by the Queen.

GRUB
The second stage of an ant's life, after the egg, but before the cocoon. Also called the larva (plural larvae).

HEAD
The front part of an ant's body, with the mouth, jaws, eyes and feelers.

HONEYDEW
A sweet, sticky liquid that aphids and similar creatures ooze from their rear ends, for ants to drink.

LARVA
A complicated name for a grub.

METAMORPHOSIS
A creature changing its shape a lot as it grows up. I did; from egg to grub, to cocoon, to me. So did Moth, who was once a caterpillar.

NECTAR
A sweet, sticky liquid that flowers make for us ants and similar creatures, such as bees and wasps, to drink.

PHEROMONES
Trails or signals that ants can't see, but which we can smell or detect. Different pheromones make ants do certain things, like forage for food, repair the nest or attack invading enemies.

PUPA
A complicated name for a cocoon.

THORAX
The middle part of an ant's body, including the legs (and in some ants, wings too).